PAUL PETERSEN

FRANK &
FEARLESS

20 BAD HABITS WHEN WRITING FOR GOVERNMENT AND HOW TO FIX THEM

Published in 2026 by Echo Books

Echo Books is an imprint of Superscript Publishing Pty Ltd.
ABN 76 644 812 395
35 Keeley Lane, Princes Hill, Victoria, 3054
www.echobooks.com.au

ISBN: 978-1-923441-24-8 (paperback)

CONTENTS

This book was written in Canberra, which is Ngunnawal Country. We acknowledge the continuing connection of the Ngunnawal people with the lands of Canberra and the Australian Capital Territory.

INTRODUCTION

MOST PEOPLE WHO work in government are required to write. It might not be the most important part of the job, but you can't avoid it. In some cases, writing will be the only contact you have with your audience. It doesn't matter whether your reader is a government minister, a senior executive, a colleague or a member of the public – you will be judged by the quality of your writing.

When writing at work, you only get one chance to communicate your message. Your reader should be able to read your document once and understand it.

Many people waste this chance because they don't know any better. Overly long and hard to read documents are accepted as normal. Inefficient review processes are tolerated despite the frustration they cause. These bad writing habits compromise the important work done by government.

Unfortunately, these habits are so common, you might not be aware of them.

In this book, we highlight 20 things you might be doing wrong when writing at work. More importantly, we show you how to fix them. Breaking these bad habits will not only improve the quality of your writing, it will save you, your managers and your readers a lot of time.

The Australian Government wants your writing to be frank and fearless, but this isn't easy. It requires confidence and an assertive writing style. The good news is that writing is a teachable skill. You might never enjoy writing but you can be good at it.

This book will teach you that skill. It will show you how to be a frank and fearless writer in government.

HABIT 1

Waiting for good guidance

YOU WON'T ALWAYS receive good guidance from managers and senior executives about your document. The guidance might be vague or contradictory, or you may get no meaningful guidance at all. This is frustrating for everyone involved and will lead to rewriting during the review process. It's also fixable with good document initiation.

Ways to initiate a document

The way you initiate a document will depend on how complex it is:

- Simple documents can be initiated with an email or verbal direction.
- Complex documents should be initiated with terms of reference or a writer's brief.

Checklists for both types of initiating guidance are in attachment A.

When to initiate a document

Too often, you will get guidance about your document during the *review* process. You write a draft but a senior executive sends it back because it missed the mark. This is avoidable. It seems obvious, but the guidance should come before you draft the document. Initiation occurs at the start of the writing process.

Who initiates a document

Every document has a sponsor. This is the person who has directed the document to be written. The document may be self-directed, or the direction may come from a more senior manager. It is the sponsor's job to provide the initiating guidance.

But document sponsors, especially if they are senior executives, are often too busy to provide adequate initiating guidance. They have a vision of what they want in the document but they don't clearly communicate this to the writer. This leads to vague guidance, which is vulnerable to misinterpretation.

If you don't get adequate initiating guidance from the document sponsor, you might need to write your own guidance. Use the checklists in attachment A to help you do this.

If you write your own initiating guidance, get the document sponsor to clear it. The sponsor owns that guidance even if you wrote it. Clearing the guidance gives the document sponsor a chance to address any confusion you might have and to put you back on the right course.

Don't wait for good guidance

Waiting for guidance is a common problem when writing for government. Don't wait – the guidance might never come, or it might

come too late. If your managers or senior executives are too busy or distracted to provide guidance, write it yourself and get them to approve it.

HABIT 2

Forgetting your reader

WHEN WRITING, IT is easy to be distracted by people who are not your intended reader. Your document might be cleared by senior executives and lawyers on its way to the reader, or it might be read by a journalist as part of a freedom of information request.

These people are not your reader. They are legitimate stakeholders, but their information needs are not the same as your reader's needs. Don't focus on these other stakeholders to the point you forget about your reader. If you try to please everyone who *might* read your document, you will irritate and confuse your reader with content they don't care about.

Satisfying other stakeholders

Focus on your reader and find a different way to satisfy other stakeholders. For example, use a covering email to provide additional background to people clearing your document. This background might be relevant to your manager but not to the reader.

You can also talk to stakeholders as part of the clearance process. It will be quicker and easier to answer their questions face-to-face than to exchange several drafts of your document.

Don't try to please everyone with one document

Some documents have more than one reader. For example, a new leave policy might be read by everyone in your agency. Each reader will have a different appetite for detail, and you won't please them all. This means compromising. If you write a policy that is overly detailed, most of your intended readers won't bother reading it all.

Other documents have only one reader. Briefs might be cleared by several people, but there is generally only one action addressee. This person is your reader, and you must focus on their needs.

If your document is getting too complicated, it is better to break it up. It is often quicker to write several documents – each with a different purpose – than to write one long complicated document. There might be overlapping content in these documents, but each will be tightly focused on its own reader.

Use structure to focus your content

Not every part of your document will get equal attention from your reader. Put your most important content in a part of your document where it can't be missed. Put less important content out of the way. If you can't bear to delete unimportant content, bury it in an attachment.

If you want to learn more about document structure, see Habits 10 and 11, where we talk about buried messages.

Don't write to yourself

Your topic is important to you, but that doesn't mean your reader has the same appetite for detail as you. If you try to impress your reader with your expertise, you are thinking more about yourself than your reader. Your priority must be to tell your reader what they need – not what you know.

HABIT 3

Shopping for evidence

MOST DOCUMENTS SOLVE a problem, and most writers have a bias towards a solution to solve that problem. This can lead writers to take shortcuts when researching and consulting. Writers tend to stop researching when they have gathered enough evidence to support their preferred solution.

This is not fair to your reader. You might be an expert on the issue, but it is your reader who is the decision-maker. They will be responsible if anything goes wrong. If you have shopped for only enough evidence to support your preferred solution, you haven't told your reader the full story.

Confirmation bias

Shopping for evidence is a sub-conscious shortcut called confirmation bias. This bias is never deliberate (that would be dishonest). You won't be aware of it when it is happening.

Confirmation bias can be reduced by making sure your research looks at all sides of an issue. Don't just consult with your usual

network. Talk to people who will challenge you. They are more likely to expose your blind spots.

This will also make your document more credible, as 2-sided arguments are more persuasive. Addressing the positives and negatives of your position will give the reader confidence that no bad surprises lie ahead.

Accuracy

The risk of getting something wrong in a rushed document is a real concern. It can embarrass the government or cause problems for executives who act upon your document. In government, there is a tension between the need for accuracy and timeliness.

Accuracy is not the same as truth. You might truthfully cite someone who is not qualified to talk about a matter, or you might write something that is true but without the context that gives it meaning. Most inaccuracy is not caused by overt lying; it is more likely to be caused by:

- using imprecise or unclear words
- overstating or understating concerns
- creating risk or problems where none really exist
- linking facts and issues when they have no real connection
- oversimplifying an issue or burying it in detail.

While government writing is not journalism, there are lessons you can learn from the media. The Reuters Handbook of Journalism provides the following guidance.

- **Correcting**. Be transparent about errors and rectify them quickly.
- **Sourcing**. Use credible sources and name them so they are responsible for the information they provide. Look for alternative views that might disprove the point you are making.

- **Reflecting reality**. Don't exaggerate your message. For example, is it really a 'significant' issue? Be precise in your descriptions.
- **Attributing**. Be honest about where your information came from. This allows the reader to make an assessment about its reliability.
- **Conveying what is necessary**. Your language should support the purpose of the document and not sanitise the message.

Being objective isn't always easy

Your reader expects you to have a clear position on your topic, but they also expect you to be objective. There will be risks and sensitivities with your proposed solution and there will be disadvantages with your recommendations. Don't forget to declare them in your document.

HABIT 4

Consulting too late

THE TOPIC YOU are writing about will *affect* people and is *affected by* people. These people are stakeholders in your document and (in most cases) should be consulted. You might even ask them to look at a draft of your document. That's a good thing to do, but it is not enough. Sending someone a draft document is *review* not *consultation*.

Your document is creating work for someone

Most government documents solve a problem – they solve *your* problem. In solving your problem, you will almost certainly create work for other people. Don't expect them to be happy about this.

Anticipate resistance by consulting with stakeholders before you start writing. Where appropriate, address or acknowledge their concerns in your document. Your reader is more likely to approve your proposed solution if they know it won't be an unwelcome surprise to stakeholders.

Use working papers for complex topics

If your document has a lot of stakeholders, you can send them working papers as part of the consultation process. Working papers aren't draft documents. They have a different purpose and give you flexibility you don't have in the final document.

Working papers are quick to write. There are no templates and you don't need to worry about formatting. Sending a working paper to stakeholders might also expose problems with your topic you weren't aware of. You can then adjust your solution to address those problems. You may even decide not to progress your document, saving you and your agency a lot of unnecessary work.

Assumptions

Research and consultation cannot go on forever. At some point you must commit to a position. You might, however, not know everything you would like to know about your topic. This requires you to make assumptions.

Assumptions are things you accept as true, but without proof. They are a substitute for facts. Assumptions normally serve you well, and they simplify the process of writing.

You won't always be aware you are making an assumption. To protect yourself from making lazy or unreasonable assumptions, write them down. This makes them explicit and more obvious to you when researching.

You don't need to declare every assumption to your reader, but you should mention the important ones. Use your professional judgement to decide what assumptions need to be declared to the reader.

Consultation occurs before you start drafting your document

You are working to a tight deadline, and you are impatient to get started writing. This is understandable but it is not efficient. Make sure your research and consultation are solid before you start drafting your document. Your research and consultation won't be perfect, and you might need to refine it later. That's ok, just do most of it *before* you start writing.

HABIT 5

Thinking your reader always cares

YOUR READER IS busy, tired and distracted. It's often late and they want to go home. Your reader is rarely enthusiastic about reading your document. They are looking at your document thinking 'why should I bother?'.

You are in a competition for your reader's attention

Your reader cannot read *every* word of *every* document they receive. They must manage time by prioritising their work. Readers look at who the document is from, the title of that document and perhaps the opening text. They then decide what to do next. Do they read it now, leave it for tomorrow or do they ignore it? These are sensible questions. It would be bad time management to read every word in every document.

Help your reader to manage time by starting with a clear purpose statement. Your purpose statement explains why the document was

sent to them and gives them a sense of how relevant, urgent and important it is. This allows a busy reader to prioritise your document.

Purpose statements must be clear

Your purpose statement must be clear. Let's define clear: **your purpose statement must be one grammatically correct sentence**. If you can't write your purpose statement as a sentence, then you probably aren't clear in your own mind about why you are writing. This means your purpose won't be clear to your reader either. The process of writing your purpose as a sentence forces you to be clear.

Place your purpose statement in an obvious position in your document. In an email, it could be your first sentence. In a longer document, it will be in your introduction. As an example, the purpose statement for this book is the last sentence of the introduction.

One purpose for one document

Keep your purpose statement confined to the document. Don't describe the background of wider issues or related topics. For example, there is a difference between the purpose of a project, and the purpose of a project report.

If you think you have more than one purpose for your document, then you should write more than one document. It is often quicker to write several shorter and more focused documents. Writing a long and complicated document is much harder and might satisfy no-one.

Purpose statements are hard to write

Your purpose statement will often be the hardest sentence to write in your document. The topic might be complex, or you might not have received good guidance from your manager

about the document. This means you might not be sure about your document's purpose.

If you are not sure about your purpose statement, don't blunder on. You will be at risk of spinning off in the wrong direction. In these cases, get your manager to clear your purpose statement. Don't let your manager get away with vague guidance – ask them to clear the *sentence* you have written. Anything other than a one sentence purpose statement is inadequate guidance and isn't fair to you.

A clear purpose saves time

Having a clear and agreed purpose for your document keeps you focused as you start developing content. It also makes sure your document will satisfy any senior managers who will clear your document. This saves time for you, your managers and your reader.

HABIT 6

Being cursed by knowledge

WHEN YOU WRITE, you have background knowledge you can't unhear or unsee. Your reader doesn't have the same background, which means what is obvious to you might not be obvious to them. This can blind you to gaps in your content because you subconsciously fill them in. This is a cognitive bias noted in 1989 by Colin Camerer, George Loewenstein and Martin Weber. They called it the *curse of knowledge*.

Breaking the curse

Your best defence against the curse of knowledge is to decide your content before you write it up. Identify your reader and list everything you think they will need to know. Consult people who can help you decide what should be on this list.

Answer the question

Most documents trigger questions in the reader's mind. Try to anticipate these questions when writing. Answering these ques-

tions will help you find the sweet spot of content – what your reader needs to know. This sweet spot is between what you know and what your reader already knows.

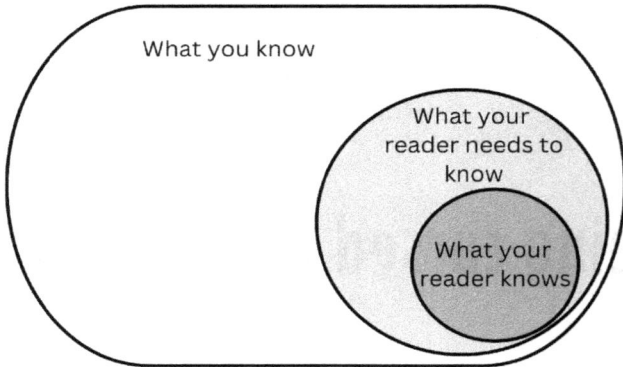

The journalist's 6 questions

Try using the journalist's 6 questions to develop a brain dump of what the reader needs to know. These 6 questions can't be answered with 'yes' or 'no'. They require a longer answer, and this makes them a good way to generate content.

The journalist's 6 questions are:

Who?	Who is affected by this issue? Who is the point of contact for this issue? Who has been consulted? Who is the delegate/person responsible for this matter?

What?	What has happened so far? What laws or policies are relevant? What options does the reader have? What do we know and what do we not know?
Where?	Where is this issue happening? Where can the reader find more information?
When?	When did this issue arise? When is action required by?
Why?	Why is the reader affected by this issue? Why is this issue important? Why has this issue emerged?
How?	How did this issue arise? How can the reader respond? How will sensitive issues be managed?

Not all these questions will be relevant to every document.

HABIT 7

Including irrelevant detail

THE CURSE OF knowledge is real and can lead writers to omit relevant information. But the opposite problem is even more common – including information your reader doesn't need. You might have included content just to be safe or because you are trying to impress your reader.

This creates a problem, as too many messages will be a flood of content that swamps your reader.

Balancing risk

It is normal to think about the risk of not telling your reader something. Your topic is important, and you want to make sure your reader has everything they need to make a good decision. But too much focus on this leads to a new risk – the risk of overwhelming your reader. When you try to tell your reader too much, you tell them nothing.

The magical number 7 plus or minus 2

How much content is too much? The answer depends on the topic, the reader, the time of day and other factors. Research by George Miller in 1956 suggests the working memory of most people can cope with 7 (plus or minus 2) chunks of information. That might be 7 numbers, 7 dot points or 7 key messages.

Other researchers have since suggested different limits, so 7 is not really a magical number. But Miller's research reminds us that our reader has limited capacity to absorb information. You can have more than 7 key messages in your document. Just don't expect your reader to remember all of them.

Think about what you can safely not tell your reader

One way to decide your key messages is to think about what your reader *doesn't* need to know. Start with your brain dump from Habit 6, then try to cut this list back.

- Cut anything that doesn't support your purpose statement. If appropriate, move it to a different document.
- Cut anything your reader already knows. This includes repetition and unnecessary background.
- Cut anything your reader can work out for themselves. This includes buzzwords, cliches, statements of the obvious and anything which is common-sense. Readers skip past this type of content until they find things they couldn't work out for themselves.

What remains after these cuts, are your key messages.

Decide your key messages before you draft your document

Decide your key messages from a brain dump, not from a draft of your document. Cutting content from a brain dump is easy, whereas cutting content from a fully drafted document is hard. Really hard.

A fully drafted document will mask duplication. Messages that are common sense will be missed because they are hidden in a paragraph. Other messages will be kept because they sound good, not because they are needed. This puts vanity ahead of clarity.

One sentence = one complete thought

The classic definition of a sentence is 'one complete thought'. Every key message listed in your brain dump is a thought. This means every message you cut from your brain dump is one less sentence you have to write. It is one less sentence that has to be reviewed. It is one less sentence that has to be read by a very busy person.

HABIT 8

Encouraging your reader

HAVE YOU EVER received an email *encouraging* you to do something (such as the annual Employee Census)? Did you prioritise time to do this or did you put it off? How many emails did you receive before you acted?

Most government documents want the reader to do something. It might be to complete a task, respond to a question or approve a request. These are all examples of a call to action, and they will be the most important words in every document you write.

Use assertive verbs

If you want your reader to do something, you need verbs. Verbs are the engines of your documents. They give your writing confidence and authority.

Not all verbs are up to this job. Soft verbs like *encourage* are unlikely to motivate a busy reader to action. In addition, soft verbs might not be interpreted by your reader the way you intended. Assertive verbs are clearer and more likely to get the result you want.

Modal verbs

Modal verbs tell the reader how serious you are about an action. The most common modal verbs used in government writing are:

must	This verb gives your reader no choice about the action. It relies on the writer's authority for weight. The verbs *is to/are required to* have the same authority.
should	This verb tells your reader to do something unless they have a good reason not to do it. Telling your reader they *should* do something is equivalent to *recommending* they do something.
may	This verb gives your reader *permission* to do something, or a *choice* about what to do.

Briefs and reports

The call to action in a brief or report will be the recommendations. Most agencies require you to build each recommendation around one of 4 core verbs.

noted/discuss	If the reader circles *noted,* this means they read what you wrote and have no questions. If they have questions, the convention is to circle *discuss.*
agreed/not agreed	If the reader circles *agreed,* this means they are not opposed to what you wrote.
approved/not approved	The verb *approve* is stronger than *agree.* If the reader circles *approved,* they have made a decision and now own the risk associated with that decision.

signed/not signed	This verb asks the reader to *sign* an attachment to the brief. This could be by hand or by digital signature.

Other core verbs can be used in other situations. For example, *endorse* is used in some reports and in committee work. It is not as common in briefs.

Don't make your reader guess what you want them to do

A good call to action uses assertive verbs that describe exactly what you want your reader to do. Choose your verbs carefully so the reader is in no doubt about what action is needed.

HABIT 9

Telling a story in every document

TELLING A STORY is the traditional approach to structuring a document. But it's not the only way to structure a document, and it's often not the best way. The modern approach is different. It gets straight to the point.

Principles of structure

You might have heard about pyramid and reverse pyramid structures, or inductive and deductive structures. These aren't principles of structure, they are ways to *think*. There is a better way to describe the principles of writing structure.

When writing, there are 2 principles of structure you should focus on:

- Flow (a traditional approach)
- Position (a modern approach)

Traditional approaches

Traditional approaches to structure are based on the smooth and logical flow of information. You start with background content and finish with the call to action. The only way the call to action makes sense is if the reader starts at the beginning and flows along until the end.

Traditional structures tell a story – like a murder mystery. You identify the murderer at the end of the book. It would make no sense to identify the murderer anywhere else.

You're not writing a murder mystery at work, but traditional structures are also good for complex topics. With complex topics, the reader needs information to allow them to understand your call to action. Providing some background and analysis will also give your reader confidence in your call to action.

Technical manuals, major reports and most policies should use a traditional structure.

Modern approaches

Modern approaches to structure don't flow. They are based on positions of emphasis.

At work, most readers don't read every part of a document. Readers spend most of their time at the start and (to a lesser extent) the end. Modern approaches to structure don't fight this. They put the most important content (the call to action) at the start of the document. In some agencies, this approach is called a bottom line up front structure.

Placing your call to action at the start of a document saves your reader time. It allows them to act without having to read the whole document.

Modern approaches to structure are good for urgent issues such as safety and security matters. They are also the best structures for busy readers. This is why the templates for most government briefs have a modern structure with the recommendations at the start.

Sensitive topics

Delivering bad news and writing about sensitive topics is never easy. These topics need an appropriate structure, especially if the reader is a colleague or member of the public. In these cases, you should use a traditional structure. Don't deliver the bad news in your first sentence. Start with enough background to give the reader time to emotionally prepare for the message.

Managers, senior executives and government ministers don't need this time. They get bad news all day, every day. They have good coping strategies. For these readers you should use a modern structure and get straight to the point. They won't like the bad news but they will appreciate the direct delivery.

HABIT 10

Burying treasure

YOUR DOCUMENT IS important but not every message in it will be of equal value. Don't bury the most important messages.

In Habit 9, we described the 2 main approaches to document structure – traditional and modern. No matter which of these approaches you use, your most important content should be at either the beginning or end of your document. Readers focus on the beginning of things and to a lesser extent, the end of things. It is the bit in the middle they are most likely to skip over. If you place important content in the middle of something, you bury it.

Structuring documents

Put your most important messages either at the beginning of the document, or next best, at the end of the document. Put less important messages in the middle sections.

In most documents, your most important content will be your call to action. This is why, in a modern approach to structure, the call to action is at the start of the document. In a traditionally struc-

tured document, the call to action is at the end. It should never be in the middle of the document.

Structuring paragraphs

The tendency for readers to skip over the middle of things also applies to your paragraphs. If you have more than one sentence in a paragraph, make the first sentence your most important one. This is called the *topic sentence*. If your most important sentence doesn't work at the start of the paragraph, make it the last sentence. This is still a position of emphasis.

Structuring sentences

Grammar is the set of rules about structuring words and sentences. We will look at some of these rules later in the book. There is, however, one rule worth mentioning here: always put the most important information in your sentence at the beginning of the sentence. This will fix many of your grammar problems. In particular, it will help you decide whether to use active or passive voice. If you bury important content in the middle of a long sentence, your grammar will become more complicated.

Make your call to action obvious

Your most important message will be your call to action, and it must be in a position of emphasis. If there is more than one action for your reader, don't sprinkle them throughout your document. Group all the actions up at either the start or the end of the document.

Reading is not a treasure hunt

It is not your reader's job to find important content. Don't make your reader search for important content by burying it in the middle of things. Place important messages where they are obvious and easy to find.

HABIT 11

Attaching important content

BUSY READERS GENERALLY won't read an attachment (or hyperlink, reference or footnote) to your document. These are useful parts of a document, but only for optional information.

Key messages must be in the main part of your document. If you put a key message in an attachment, you are telling the reader it doesn't matter if they read that content. If the reader has an appetite for more detail, they will find it, but they mostly won't bother.

Types of attachments

Attachment is a general term that includes:

- **Annexes.** Annexes contain content that amplifies, clarifies or justifies content in the main document. Annexes rely on the main document to make sense.
- **Appendixes.** Appendixes are a sub-level to an annex. They contain content that supports the annex. Some agencies use appendixes instead of annexes.

- **Enclosures.** Enclosures also support the main document, but unlike annexes and appendixes, they don't rely on the main document to make sense. They are complete documents on their own.

These definitions are becoming less important, and some agencies now just use the generic term *attachments*.

Some attachments are more important than others

In some cases, the attachment is the main document. For example, your email might be a few words used to send a document to your reader. In this situation, the attachment is the main document, and the email is just an 'envelope' to send it.

Some major reports have attachments designed for specific readers. For example, the finance attachment of a report would be the main content for readers from the finance team.

Attachments and hyperlinks can look suspicious

You can't avoid using attachments and hyperlinks, especially with emails. However, readers who don't know you might be worried about malicious content and be reluctant to open an attachment or to click on a hyperlink. In these cases, make sure your covering email has enough content to allow the reader to do what is required of them.

Hyperlinks have a short shelf-life

Hyperlinks are convenient but they don't last forever. If you have a hyperlink in your document, make sure it works. Set the hyperlink to a main page that will endure. Hyperlinks should also be set to open in a new page.

For documents with a long shelf-life, you might be better to use an attachment instead.

Attachments are legally binding but they aren't always fair

Attachments are often used to satisfy legal requirements in contracts and similar documents. Terms and conditions are generally in attachments, and very few people read them before signing the contract. Despite this, placing terms and conditions in an attachment still makes them legally binding.

Long, hard to read attachments might be legally binding, but that doesn't mean they are best practice. Good writers do everything they can to make a document easy for the reader. This means taking essential content from attachments and including it in the main document.

Don't expect people to read your attachments. It's not always fair to your reader.

HABIT 12

Looking unprofessional

FORMATTING IS ABOUT a document's appearance and is shaped by agency style guides and templates. Your agency and your reader expect your documents to look professional. There are some simple things you can do to achieve this.

Use generous white space

Dense blocks of text can look like a grey wall to readers. White space breaks this up and will improve the appearance of your document. You can create white space by inserting headings and by not crimping margins.

Don't justify your text

Justified text is where each line is spaced so both left and right sides of a page are aligned. This creates unnatural spaces between words and is harder to read. In some documents, it can also create distracting 'rivers' through your pages and paragraphs.

Minimise capital letters

Too many capital letters are distracting and hard to read. Capital letters are used for proper nouns, and their overuse can confuse readers about what is important. Using all capitals is also the equivalent of shouting at your reader.

The modern trend is to minimise use of capital letters. Capital letters are used in some abbreviations and for the first letter of:

- sentences
- headings
- proper nouns
- important words in titles.

Headings

Headings are signposts for your document. They help your reader to navigate your content and to find the information they are interested in.

Good headings should be:

- **Accurate**. Main headings and the subject lines of emails should match the purpose of your document.
- **Unique**. Avoid repeating headings in a document. Headings should match the unique content that follows.
- **Meaningful**. Use words a reader would enter into a search engine to find your content.
- **Consistent**. Use the same level of heading for blocks of content of similar importance.
- **Attractive**. Keep headings to one line. Longer headings, especially if they are capitalised, are jarring and hard to read.
- **Accessible**. Don't turn 'normal' text into a heading by changing it to bold or a larger size. Use heading styles in Microsoft Word to create true headings. This ensures the headings in your document are accessible to screen readers.

Use sentence case or title case for headings. Sentence case capitalises the first word of the heading and any proper nouns. For example:

Essential writing skills: emails and letters

Title case capitalises the first word of the heading and the important words. For example:

Essential Writing Skills: Emails and Letters

Use of sentence case or title case is based on your agency's style guide, not your personal preference.

HABIT 13

Trying to impress your reader

LONG WORDS ARE often used in a misguided attempt to sound more official or impressive. For example:

*The proposed development is **in the vicinity of** your property.*

Instead of a shorter and simpler word:

> *The proposed development is **near** your property.*

Your reader won't be impressed by fancy words, they are more likely to be annoyed.

They will also be annoyed if you use foreign words, jargon, abbreviations and unnecessary technical language. When choosing words, you should:

- choose the shortest words that meet your intent
- use a few simple words instead of a single long complex word.

Nominalisations (fake verbs)

Government writing is infested with nominalisations. This is where a verb is changed to a noun, with extra words then added to describe the action. These nominalisations are 'fake verbs'. They are another misguided attempt to make a document sound more impressive. For example:

The Director **made the decision** *to extend the project.*

Instead of a direct verb:

The Director **decided** *to extend the project.*

Fake verbs aren't always bad. They can be used to soften tone, and sometimes the direct verb looks wrong. For example:

During the interview, applicants may
ask questions of *the panel.*

This is a fake verb, but it is better than the oddly phrased direct alternative:

During the interview, applicants may **question** *the panel.*

Adjectives and adverbs

Adjectives and adverbs describe or modify nouns and verbs. They tell us something more about the noun or verb.

Overuse of adjectives and adverbs are another example of trying too hard to impress the reader. For example:

We **formally** *request your comments about the proposal.*

In this example, it is not clear what *formally* means. The adverb adds no value to the sentence. The overuse of adjectives and adverbs dilutes their impact.

Fake verbs, adjectives and adverbs aren't always bad. You should use them when they add clarity to your writing. Don't use them out of habit.

Technical language, jargon and abbreviations

Technical language, jargon and abbreviations are fine for readers who are familiar with them. Readers who aren't familiar with them deserve plain language instead. This might mean using more words to get your point across. For example:

*I'm concerned about **honesty and ethics**.*

not

*I'm concerned about **probity**.*

Don't try to impress your reader by using technical language, jargon or abbreviations to prove you are an expert. Only someone who understands a complex topic can describe it using plain language.

HABIT 14

Making people read things twice

HAVE YOU EVER struggled to understand a document? Have you ever had to re-read something (perhaps several times) and found yourself getting progressively more frustrated and annoyed?

Your reader should never have to read something more than once to understand it. Never.

Readability

The concept of making something easy to read is called readability. Readability is determined by the length of your words and sentences. Long words and sentences require greater effort to process, and this makes them harder to read. Fortunately, there is a tool in Microsoft Word to help you check the readability of your documents.

Checking readability

You will need to activate the readability tool in Microsoft Word the first time you use it.

Follow this menu path to do this:

File > Options > Proofing > Check 'show readability statistics'

Once readability statistics are activated, Microsoft Word will provide those statistics whenever you use Microsoft Editor (in older versions of Word, this is the spelling and grammar checker).

There are 2 readability scores in Microsoft Word:

• **Flesch reading ease**. This rates text on a 100-point scale. The higher the score, the easier it is to understand the text.
• **Flesch-Kincaid grade level**. This rates text on a school grade level. For example, an 8th grader can understand text that has a grade level of 8.0.

Recommended readability levels

Most agencies use the Flesch-Kincaid grade level instead of the Flesch reading ease score. The Australian Government Style Manual recommends a Flesch-Kincaid grade level of 7. While this grade level is appropriate for some readers, it is unrealistic for many government documents. The following grade levels are more achievable and will meet the needs of most agencies.

A letter to a member of the public.	8 to 10
An email to a colleague at work.	8 to 12
A document posted to a website.	6 to 8
An email to a senior executive.	8 to 10

As a benchmark, the Flesch-Kincaid grade level of this book is 7.2.

Improving readability

You can improve the readability of your document by:

* removing unnecessary words
* replacing long words with shorter and simpler words
* adding full stops to reduce sentence length.

Shown below is an example of how these 3 steps can transform a sentence.

Original sentence

The subject application will be on exhibition for 14 days from Wednesday, 3 August 2025 until Tuesday, 16 August 2025 at the Division's principal office at the Customer Service Counter, ground floor, Civic Centre - corner of Smith Street and Green Place - during ordinary office hours, being 9.00 am to 5.00 pm Monday to Friday.

54 words Flesch-Kincaid grade level: 26

Step one: Remove unnecessary words

The ~~subject~~ application will be on exhibition ~~for 14 days~~ from ~~Wednesday,~~ ~~3 August 2025~~ until ~~Tuesday,~~ 16 August 2025 at the ~~Division's principal office at the~~ Customer Service Counter, ~~ground floor, Civic Centre -~~ corner of Smith Street and Green Place ~~- during ordinary office hours, being~~ 9.00 am to 5.00 pm Monday to Friday.

32 words Flesch-Kincaid grade level: 16.2

Step 2: Replace long words with simple words.

*The application will be **on exhibition** from 3 **until** 16 August 2025 at our **Customer Service Counter, corner of Smith Street and Green Place**, 9.00 am to 5.00 pm Monday to Friday.*

With simpler words and phrasing

*The application will be **displayed** from 3 **to** 16 August 2025 at our **office, 126 Smith Street**, **9 am** to **5 pm** Monday to Friday.*

25 words Flesch-Kincaid grade level: 12.5

Step 3: Add full stops (one sentence = one thought)

We will display the application at our office at 126 Smith Street from 3 to 16 August 2025. The counter is open Monday to Friday from 9 am to 5 pm.

Average 15.5 words per sentence Flesch-Kincaid grade level: 8.7

One sentence = one thought

Commas are useful, but too many commas are a sign of an overly complicated sentence. It is often better to break a sentence up than to add commas to it.

The classic definition of a sentence is 'one complete thought'. Having too many thoughts in a sentence will make it longer and harder to read. Keep your sentences shorter and easier to read by making sure each sentence is limited to one complete thought.

Accessibility

Readability is different to accessibility. Accessibility ensures your document can be understood by readers from diverse back-

grounds. This includes people who rely on technology such as screen readers.

Please refer to the Australian Government Style Manual if you would like to know more about accessibility. You can also attend one of the courses on this topic run by Vision Australia.

HABIT 15

Worrying about grammar

SOME PEOPLE ARE passionate about grammar and have fixed views about it. You have more important things to do at work than argue with them. Here is some simple guidance to get you through that work.

Active and passive voice

Active and passive voice are grammatical terms about the structure of sentences. Governments prefer active voice sentences because they are more accountable than passive voice sentences. Active voice sentences make it clear not just what was done, but also who did it.

An active voice sentence places the person or thing that performs an action in front of the verb. For example:

The director signed the project report this morning. (active)

Anything other than this order is called passive voice. For example:

The project report was signed by the
director this morning. (passive)

Some sentences omit the 'doer' completely. These are called agentless passive sentences. For example:

The project report was signed this morning. (agentless passive)

Be careful with agentless passive sentences because they reduce accountability. The next sentence is agentless passive, and it isn't clear who is responsible for briefing the team.

The team is to be briefed about the new
structure as soon as possible.

Readability is more important than grammar

These examples were simple sentences. It was easy to identify which sentences were active and passive. It won't be as easy with long and complex sentences.

The solution is to improve readability before worrying about grammar. Improving the readability of your sentences will often fix their grammar. If it doesn't fix the grammar, the sentence will be simple enough for you to.

We saw this in an earlier example in this book (shown again below). The original sentence is hard to read. It is a grammatical mess with 5 commas and 2 dashes. It's not clear whether the sentence is active or passive voice.

The subject application will be on exhibition
for 14 days from Wednesday, 3 August
2025 until Tuesday, 16 August 2025 at the
Division's principal office at the Customer

Service Counter, ground floor, Civic Centre - corner of Smith Street and Green Place - during ordinary office hours, being 9.00 am to 5.00 pm Monday to Friday.

The readable version fixed the grammar. It is 2 active voice sentences and has no commas.

We will display the application at our office at 126 Smith Street from 3 to 16 August 2025. The counter is open Monday to Friday from 9 am to 5 pm.

Structure is also important

Active voice isn't always better. Passive voice is softer tone and might take the edge off a harsh message. Passive voice is also better when the 'doer' is less important than the object of the action. In this next example, the passive voice sentence is better because it focuses on the Minister:

An adviser will accompany the Minister during the visit. (active)

The Minister will be accompanied by an adviser during the visit. (passive)

Remember the principles of structure and put your most important information at the beginning of the sentence. It's ok if that makes it a passive voice sentence.

You can't ignore grammar but don't focus on it. Improve your readability first. Your grammar will then be easier to manage.

HABIT 16

Being too polite

FRANK AND FEARLESS writing requires frank and fearless tone. It is easy to adjust tone when you speak to someone face-to face. You can use body language, facial expression and voice to adjust tone. When writing, you have none of these tools. It is hard to adjust tone when writing

Government writing should use assertive tone

The good news is you don't need to adjust tone as much as you think. All government writing should use an assertive tone. This tone balances being direct and being polite.

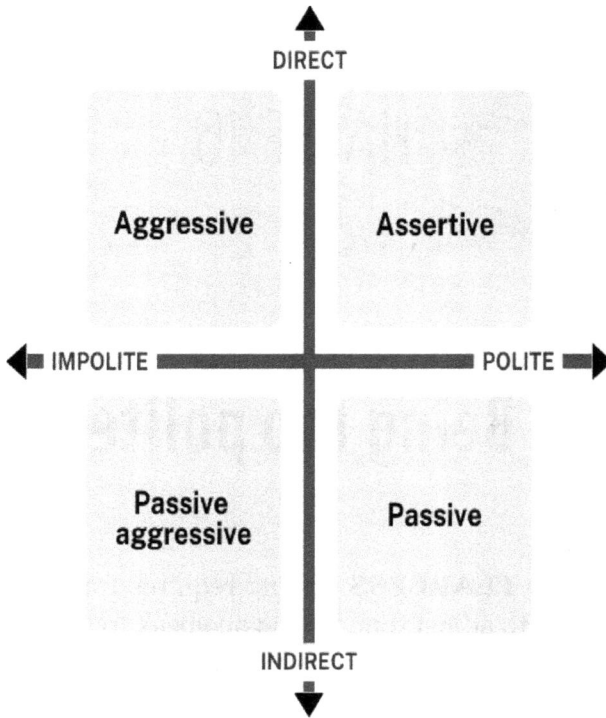

Other tones are never acceptable:

- Aggressive tone is direct but has no consideration for the feelings of the reader. Aggressive tone is rude and in extreme cases is misconduct.
- Passive tone tries too hard to avoid causing offence. This can muddy the message and confuse the reader.
- Passive aggressive tone is neither direct nor polite. It often masks a negative intent with pleasant language. Sarcasm is an example of passive aggressive tone.

Being frank and fearless is hard

Assertive tone is appropriate even when writing about sensitive issues, such as delivering bad news to your reader. There is some

room for adjustment, but not as much as you think. Delivering bad news is never easy, but you owe your reader respectful and honest delivery of that news.

If you are a naturally passive writer, using an assertive tone will feel uncomfortable. Be ready for this psychological hurdle. Get a second opinion from a colleague if you are worried your phrasing is too direct. This will give you the confidence to write more assertively.

Improving readability improves tone

It is unlikely you will use an aggressive tone in your writing, as it tends to be obvious. It is more likely you will make the opposite mistake of using an overly passive tone. You might be trying so hard to avoid offending your reader that you are not direct enough with them.

If this has happened, improving the readability of your sentences will shift your tone from passive to assertive. Get rid of the fluff words, swap the fancy words for simpler words. Most importantly, build your sentences around one main thought. When you do this, your writing will still be respectful. It will also be frank and fearless.

HABIT 17

Multitasking during review

EVERY DOCUMENT SHOULD be reviewed at least twice – once for the substance of the document and once for the style of the document.

Substance and style reviews look at very different things. If you multitask by trying to do them at the same time, your focus will keep shifting. This increases the risk of missing something important.

Substance review

The substance review is about the content and structure of your document. It involves checking the document provides enough information to the reader to achieve its purpose. The substance review looks at:

- **Purpose.** Has the purpose of the document been clearly stated? Is it written as a sentence and up front in the document?
- **Relevant key messages.** Do the key messages support the purpose statement? Are there any irrelevant messages that should be deleted or moved to a different document?

- **Call to action.** Is the call to action accurate and assertive? Does it use the correct verbs and is it consistent with the purpose of the document?
- **Structure.** Does the document have a structure that either flows or gets straight to the main point? Have any important messages been buried? Should any messages be moved to an attachment or should any messages in attachments be moved to the main document?

Style review

The style review makes sure the document is easy to read and correctly formatted. It looks at:

- **Plain English.** Are there any words which should be replaced by simpler words? Are there any fake verbs, adjectives or adverbs which should be deleted or replaced?
- **Readability.** What is the Flesch-Kincaid grade level of the document? Is it appropriate for the reader?
- **Grammar and punctuation.** Does the document prefer active voice to passive voice? Is there too much punctuation?
- **Tone.** Is the tone assertive (polite and direct)?
- **Spelling.** Are there any spelling mistakes?
- **Format.** Does the document use the right template? Does it use the correct formatting conventions for your agency?

Attachment B contains checklists for substance and style reviews.

Review substance and style separately

Substance and style reviews check different things and require different approaches.

Substance reviews focus on *what* was said and *where* it was said. This requires an understanding of the topic, especially if it is a

technical matter. They might also be done by several people, sometimes at the same time.

Style reviews focus on *how* the document was phrased. This requires an eye for detail and an understanding of readability. In a best-case scenario, you might need only one style review.

HABIT 18

Hoping for clearance

CLEARANCE PROCESSES ARE needed to ensure account-ability in government. But these processes are often inefficient and frustrating. Too often, we hope our document will survive the clearance process. *Hope* is not good enough – you must *manage* the review process.

Review substance before style

Check substance and structure before worrying about style. There is no point looking at word choice, spelling, tone and grammar in a section of a document you later decide isn't required.

Complex documents might need more than one person to review their substance. These might be subject matter experts, senior managers or other stakeholders. Reconcile their feedback about substance before worrying about style issues.

Give your reviewers a specific job

When reviewing, the freshest eyes belong to someone other than the writer. If you ask someone else to review a document, tell them which review you want them to do – substance or style. If you don't tell them, you will probably get a focus on style. This is because reviewing style is easier than reviewing substance.

Tell managers, executives and subject matter experts to focus on reviewing substance not style. You are interested in their feedback about the content of your document. Their opinions on punctuation are less important.

Reassure substance reviewers that you will fix grammar and punctuation issues when the content is cleared. This frees them to focus on substance.

If you ask someone to do a substance review, they may not know what you mean unless they have read this book. You should explain their task using the checklists at attachment B.

Follow up your reviewers

Don't be passive if your manager or a subject matter expert gives you feedback about style instead of substance. They were probably tired or distracted and took the easy option.

This is understandable, but they haven't done their job. Fix any style issues they identify but then follow up. Ask if they have any comments about the document's substance. A good reviewer will recognise what happened and give you the feedback you need.

Put your document in the freezer

If you are reviewing your own writing, put it in the freezer. This means setting it aside for as long as you can between writing and

reviewing. You will pick up problems in your writing that you would otherwise have missed. Overnight in the freezer is good but a few days is better.

If your deadline is urgent, make a cup of coffee. A few minutes in the freezer between writing and reviewing is better than no time in the freezer.

HABIT 19

Tracking too many changes

TRACK CHANGES IS part of the *Review* function in Microsoft Word. It has its place, but not when reviewing the substance of a document. Tracking changes invites a reviewer to change your words. That is part of a style review, not a substance review.

Use comments for the substance review

For substance, you want comments. Ask reviewers to use the comments function in Microsoft Word instead of track changes. Comments are more efficient than track changes when providing feedback about substance.

If your reviewer is still likely to use track changes, convert the document to pdf format. Your reviewers can use the comments function in Adobe Reader, or you can give them a separate sheet for their comments.

Better still, give/get feedback about substance face-to-face. This allows for questions and answers. For complex documents, you might hold a meeting with stakeholders to get their feedback. This

will be much quicker than exchanging emails, because conflicting views can be worked through in person. It also allows you to keep the reviewers focused on their task if they become distracted by minor style issues.

Control who reviews a document

It is common for more than one person to review documents for substance. There might be several subject matter experts involved, or several levels of management clearing the document. All these people should be focused on substance not style.

This is another reason to use comments instead of track changes for substance reviews. You do not want 5 track changed documents coming back to you. You will never merge them. You want 5 sets of comments. These will be much easier to reconcile.

Don't fix everything you find

It is not the job of your manager to fix every spelling mistake in your document. If an error has been repeated in a document, ask them to identify one usage so you can fix it throughout the document.

If you are reviewing a colleague's document, use a light touch. Too many mark-ups during review can overwhelm the writer. If you change everything a colleague writes, they won't put much effort into future work.

HABIT 20

Editing for vanity

YOUR WRITING MUST serve your reader, not you. Don't include something because **you** think it is important. Don't use words because **you** think they sound good. You must think about what is important to the reader and what will sound good to them. The same principles apply when reviewing a document.

Don't over-review a document just to suit your personal preferences. You might think 'happy' is a better word than 'glad' but no-one else cares. These types of changes are called vanity editing and they are unnecessary work.

False rules

There are a lot of false rules about writing in English. For example, you might have been told you are not allowed to start a sentence with words like *but* and *because*. This is not a rule and never has been.

Don't be too prescriptive about language rules. English is a complex and flexible language with a lot of rules and a lot of exceptions to those rules.

Don't skip the spell-check

Spelling mistakes are unprofessional and will distract many readers. Your reader might not trust your content if you don't get the small things right.

Don't guess the spelling of a word. The spell-checker in Microsoft Word isn't perfect, but you should still be using it.

Don't guess the meaning of a word

Some words sound similar but mean different things. For example, *ensure* means something different to *insure*.

If you are unsure about the meaning of a word, don't use it. Your reader is also unlikely to know what the word means, and they might guess a different meaning to you. It is better to use a few simple words instead of a single less familiar word. Your reader should never need to use a dictionary to understand what you wrote.

Know what good enough means

Some documents need extra levels of quality control. Strategic policies and ministerial-level documents require careful attention to word choice and senior executives may direct these types of changes.

Other documents need fewer changes. For less important topics, resist the urge to impose your voice on the document. You should only change something if the change improves clarity.

For example, perhaps the writer used the word *utilise* in the document. That would normally be wrong – *use* is a better word than *utilise*. But let it go if that is the only problem you pick up in the document. *Utilise* is a clear word, and the reader can cope with the occasional long word if it is clear.

CONCLUSION

WHAT YOU DO in government is important. This means what you write is important as well. Which means your writing should be good. This book has shown you what good writing looks like.

Good writing isn't always easy to do. It requires tough decisions about content and the moral courage to use assertive tone. Bad writing habits make this even harder. Habits are hard to break but the 20 habits described in this book are worth breaking.

You might not need to do everything in this book. Focus on the habits that are most relevant to you. If you overcome even one bad writing habit, you will save time for yourself, your colleagues and your readers.

Frank and fearless writing is essential to good government. It's not always easy, but it is achievable.

ATTACHMENTS

ATTACHMENT A: INITIATING GUIDANCE

INITIATING GUIDANCE SETS out the purpose, scope, timings and responsibilities associated with a document. Simple documents can be initiated verbally or with an email. Complex documents need more detailed initiating guidance.

SMART criteria for simple documents

For simple documents such as briefs, use these SMART criteria.

Specific	What type of document is required? Who will be the writer(s) and sponsor?
Measurable	What is the purpose of this document? How will you know if it achieves that purpose? What will you be looking for when you review a draft?
Achievable	Do the writers have the time, knowledge and experience to write this document? Are relevant stakeholders available for consultation?
Relevant	Is the document important enough to justify the work required to write and clear it? What priority have you allocated to this work?

| **Time** | When is the document needed by the reader? |
| **bound** | What milestones need to be met along the way? |

Terms of reference and writer's briefs

The convention inside most agencies is to initiate reports with terms of reference and to initiate policies with writer's briefs. You should think about the following points when drafting terms of reference and writer's briefs:

- Identify the document sponsor. Who will clear and release it?
- Define the purpose of the document. Write this as a sentence.
- Specify the level and scope of the document:

  - Who is the reader?
  - What matters are to be covered?
  - What matters are to be excluded?
  - What action is required of the reader?

- Explain the need for the document, including relevant background.
- Specify the type of document and how it will be distributed.
- Allocate responsibilities for document production, especially who will do the research, writing and reviewing.
- Identify relevant information sources, including relevant references.
- Identify stakeholders. Who should be consulted before writing, and who should be asked to review drafts.
- Specify key production dates. When is the first draft due and when is the final draft due?
- Specify any constraints on the document. For example, is it classified or subject to special handling requirements?
- Specify any non-standard writing conventions or styles.
- Allocate resources to produce the document. Describe the support available to the writer and the priority of this work.

ATTACHMENT B: REVIEW CHECKLISTS

Substance review	
Purpose	Is the purpose of the document clear (one sentence)?
	Is the purpose stated up front?
Key messages	Is every message relevant to the purpose?
	Are any messages repeated?
	Are any messages common sense or statements of the obvious?
	Should any messages be moved to a different document or to an attachment?
Call to action	Do action statements include identity, verb and action?
	Are the verbs accurate and assertive?

Substance review	
Structure	Does the document have a logical structure that either flows or gets straight to the main point?
	Are any important messages buried in the middle of something?
	Does the document make sense without having to read any attachments?

Style review	
Plain English	Does the document use words that will be familiar to the reader?
	Does the document minimise use of abbreviations, technical language and jargon?
Readability	Does the document have an appropriate Flesch–Kincaid grade level?
	Is each sentence based on one main thought?
Grammar	Does the document prefer active voice?
	Is passive voice used only where it improves tone or meaning?
Spelling and punctuation	Are there any spelling mistakes?
	Does the document contain too much punctuation?
Tone	Does the document use assertive tone (polite and direct)?
Accessibility	If necessary, has the document been checked for accessibility?
Format	Does the document use the correct template?
	Should the document have a protective marking?

ACKNOWLEDGEMENTS

Reuters Journalistic Standards. Available at https://reuter-sagency.com/about/standards-values/

Camerer, Loewenstein & Weber. The curse of knowledge in economic settings: An experimental analysis. *Journal of Political Economy* 97(5) (1989)

George Miller. The Magical Number Seven, Plus or Minus Two: Some Limits on our Capacity for Processing Information, *Psychological Review* 63 (1956)

Australian Government Style Manual. Available at https://www.stylemanual.gov.au

WRITING TRAINING

Petersen Ink is an Australian business that delivers writing, editing and training services to business and government. Our face-to-face writing courses are among the most popular courses offered to government employees.

Essential writing skills: Emails and letters. This is our foundation course, designed for people who write routine correspondence. It is a good course for APS and ASO levels 1 to 4

Essential writing skills: Briefs and reports. This is our most popular course and is designed for people who write documents that support action and decision-making. It is a good course for APS and ASO levels 5 to 6.

Essential writing skills: Managers and executives. This is our top-level course and is suitable for managers who are either writing or managing others who write. It is a good option for executive levels 1/2 and senior officer grades, or for people preparing for those levels.

Essential writing skills: Editing and review. This course is for people where reviewing documents is a large part of their work. Each course is tailored for the group of participants.

We also offer an online self-paced writing program. This training can be done at work or at home, on a computer, tablet or phone. The program provides 12 months access to materials. In that time, learners can stop, re-start or repeat lessons as often as they like.

See our website if you would like to know more about our training courses.

www.petersenink.com.au

www.ingramcontent.com/pod-product-compliance
Lightning Source LLC
Chambersburg PA
CBHW072043040426
42447CB00012BB/3001